Ultimate

Mises

Browser Bible

The Essential A-Z
Handbook for Everyone

Jerry P. G. Bill

TABLE OF CONTENTS

Ultimate Mises Browser Bible

Ultimate Mises Browser Bible

Ultimate Mises Browser Bible

Introduction to the Mises Browser

The Mises Browser is a revolutionary web browsing tool designed to integrate decentralization, privacy, and cryptocurrency functionality into one seamless platform. Its focus on Web3 capabilities makes it a standout choice for individuals who value secure, efficient, and innovative ways to interact with the internet.

What Is the Mises Browser?

The Mises Browser is a cutting-edge web browser built to cater specifically to the needs of the Web3 ecosystem. It combines the functionalities of traditional web browsers with advanced tools for blockchain interaction, cryptocurrency management, and decentralized application (dApp) accessibility.

Core Features:

- **Privacy First:** The browser blocks trackers, ads, and other intrusive elements by default, ensuring a secure and private browsing experience.
- **Web3 Integration:** It allows users to seamlessly access blockchain-based applications and services, offering native support for cryptocurrencies and dApps.
- **Crypto Wallet:** Built directly into the browser, the cryptocurrency wallet facilitates secure transactions without the need for third-party plugins.
- **User-Friendly Design:** Despite its advanced features, the browser maintains an intuitive interface, making it accessible for both novice and experienced users.

In essence, the Mises Browser bridges the gap between the traditional internet and the decentralized web, empowering users to take control of their online presence while staying at the forefront of technology.

History and Evolution

The Mises Browser emerged as a response to growing concerns over privacy violations, centralization of internet services, and the increasing demand for decentralized tools. Its development can be traced through several pivotal phases:

1. **The Idea Phase:**
   As blockchain technology gained prominence in the late 2010s, the need for a browser that could handle the unique requirements of decentralized applications became evident. Developers began brainstorming how to create a tool that would empower users to engage with

blockchain technologies effortlessly.

2. **Initial Development and Launch:**
   The first version of the Mises Browser was launched in the early 2020s. It introduced basic Web3 features, including support for Ethereum-based dApps and a built-in wallet. Early adopters praised its simplicity and security, helping it quickly gain traction among blockchain enthusiasts.

3. **Rapid Growth and Feature Expansion:**
   Over time, the browser underwent significant updates, adding support for multiple blockchains, improving wallet functionalities, and enhancing speed and privacy features. Partnerships with Web3 developers and blockchain organizations further solidified its position as a leader in decentralized browsing.

4. **Integration of Decentralized Identity and Advanced Security:**

In recent iterations, the browser began incorporating decentralized identity solutions, allowing users to control their digital identities without relying on centralized authorities. Additionally, enhancements in encryption and anti-tracking technologies have made the Mises Browser one of the most secure options available.

5. **Mainstream Adoption:**
   Today, the Mises Browser is not just a tool for blockchain enthusiasts but also a powerful option for everyday users seeking privacy and efficiency. Its integration with decentralized finance (DeFi) platforms and NFT marketplaces has made it a go-to browser for navigating the future of the internet.

Why the Mises Browser Matters

The importance of the Mises Browser lies in its ability to address several critical challenges and opportunities in the modern digital landscape:

1. **Empowering Privacy:**
   In an age where user data is commodified, the Mises Browser offers a safe haven by blocking trackers and anonymizing browsing behavior. Users no longer need to compromise their privacy for convenience.

2. **Driving Decentralization:**
   The centralized internet, dominated by a handful of tech giants, has been criticized for censorship, monopolistic practices, and data exploitation. The Mises Browser champions decentralization, giving power back to the users and promoting a fairer internet.

3. **Facilitating Cryptocurrency Adoption:**
   With cryptocurrencies becoming mainstream, tools that simplify their use

are crucial. The Mises Browser's built-in wallet and seamless integration with crypto platforms lower the barrier to entry for new users and enhance the experience for seasoned investors.

4. **Enhancing Accessibility to Web3:** Decentralized applications have the potential to transform industries like finance, healthcare, and gaming. The Mises Browser makes these tools accessible, paving the way for mass adoption of blockchain technology.

5. **Future-Proofing Online Interactions:** As the internet evolves toward decentralization and blockchain-driven innovations, the Mises Browser positions itself as an essential tool for staying ahead of the curve. Its forward-thinking design ensures users are ready to embrace the next generation of online experiences.

Getting Started with the Mises Browser

The Mises Browser is designed to make your entry into the Web3 world as seamless as possible. Whether you're a beginner or an experienced user of blockchain technologies, getting started with the Mises Browser is straightforward. Below, we provide a comprehensive guide covering installation, system requirements, and initial configuration to help you unlock the full potential of this innovative browser.

Installation Guide

Installing the Mises Browser is a quick and hassle-free process. Follow these steps to get started:

1. **Visit the Official Website:**

   - Navigate to the official Mises Browser website (e.g., www.misesbrowser.com) to ensure you're downloading a legitimate and secure version. Avoid third-party sites to protect your device from malware.

2. **Choose Your Platform:**

   - The Mises Browser supports a variety of platforms, including:
     - **Desktop:** Windows, macOS, and Linux
     - **Mobile:** Android and iOS
     - **Tablet:** Compatible versions for Android and iPads
   - Select the version appropriate for your device.

3. **Download the Installer:**

   ○ Click the **Download** button to
     obtain the installer. The file size is
     typically small, ensuring a swift
     download even on slower
     connections.

4. **Run the Installer:**

   ○ Locate the downloaded file and
     open it. Follow the on-screen
     instructions to begin the
     installation.
   ○ On desktop devices, you may be
     prompted to select a destination
     folder for the browser installation.

5. **Grant Permissions:**

   ○ Depending on your device, you
     may need to grant certain
     permissions, such as allowing
     installations from unknown sources
     on Android or bypassing macOS

security settings for third-party applications.

6. **Launch the Browser:**

   o Once installed, launch the browser to complete the setup process.

System Requirements

To ensure smooth operation and compatibility, your device must meet the following system requirements:

1. **Desktop:**

   o **Operating System:** Windows 10 or higher, macOS 10.12 (Sierra) or later, or Linux (Ubuntu 18.04+ or equivalent)
   o **Processor:** Intel Core i3 or equivalent (64-bit processor)

- ○ **RAM:** 4GB minimum (8GB recommended for optimal performance)
- ○ **Storage Space:** 500MB free disk space
- ○ **Graphics:** Basic integrated graphics sufficient

2. **Mobile (Android and iOS):**

- ○ **Operating System:** Android 8.0 or later, iOS 12.0 or later
- ○ **Processor:** Quad-core processor or higher
- ○ **RAM:** 2GB minimum (3GB recommended)
- ○ **Storage Space:** 200MB free space

3. **Tablet:**

- ○ Ensure compatibility with the Android or iPadOS version as specified under the mobile requirements.

4. **Internet Connection:**

- A stable internet connection is required for Web3 interactions, blockchain integration, and updates.

By meeting these requirements, you'll ensure the Mises Browser runs efficiently, offering a seamless browsing experience.

Initial Configuration

Once the Mises Browser is installed, it's time to customize it to suit your preferences and maximize its functionality. Follow these steps to configure the browser:

1. **Set Up Your Default Settings:**

   - Upon first launch, the browser will prompt you to choose default settings for language, search engine, and privacy preferences.
   - Select your desired language and customize the privacy settings to match your security needs.

2. **Create or Import a Wallet:**

   ○ The browser features a built-in cryptocurrency wallet. You can either:
      ■ **Create a New Wallet:** Follow the guided steps to generate a new wallet. Store your recovery phrase securely, as it is critical for regaining access to your funds.
      ■ **Import an Existing Wallet:** Use your existing wallet's seed phrase to integrate it with the browser.

3. **Sync Across Devices:**

   ○ If you plan to use the Mises Browser on multiple devices, enable synchronization. This feature ensures your bookmarks, wallet, and browsing history are accessible on all connected devices.

4. **Customize the Homepage:**

   ○ The homepage serves as your gateway to the internet. Personalize it by:
     - Adding your favorite dApps, blockchain networks, or frequently visited sites.
     - Selecting a preferred theme or layout for visual appeal.

5. **Enable Security Features:**

   ○ Access the settings menu to enable advanced privacy and security options, such as:
     - Tracker and ad blocking
     - Enhanced encryption for wallet transactions
     - VPN or proxy integration for anonymous browsing

6. **Install Extensions:**

   ○ If you need additional tools, visit the Mises Browser extension store.

Popular extensions include productivity tools, blockchain analytics, and Web3 utilities.

7. **Explore Web3 and dApps:**

   o Use the browser's Web3 features to connect with decentralized applications, interact with blockchain networks, or trade on decentralized exchanges. The browser's built-in support for Ethereum, Binance Smart Chain, and other blockchains ensures seamless interactions.

8. **Test the Browser:**

   o Spend some time navigating the interface, testing features like multiple tabs, private browsing mode, and wallet transactions to familiarize yourself with the environment.

By following this comprehensive guide, you'll be well-prepared to explore the full potential of the Mises Browser. Its robust feature set and user-centric design ensure that your journey into the decentralized web is both smooth and rewarding. Whether you're browsing, investing, or exploring Web3 technologies, the Mises Browser offers the tools you need for a secure and efficient experience.

Key Features of the Mises Browser

The Mises Browser has become a go-to tool for users navigating the evolving digital landscape, offering an impressive suite of features that combine cutting-edge technology with user-friendly design. Its capabilities address critical concerns such as privacy, security, speed, and Web3 integration. Below, we delve into its most notable features:

Privacy-Centric Browsing

Privacy is at the core of the Mises Browser's design philosophy. In a world where data breaches and invasive tracking are rampant, the browser offers robust tools to protect user anonymity and security.

1. **No Data Collection:**

   o Unlike traditional browsers that collect and monetize user data, the Mises Browser operates on a strict no-data-collection policy. It ensures your browsing history, search queries, and personal information are not stored or shared with third parties.

2. **Built-In VPN Support:**

   o The browser includes native VPN integration, allowing users to browse the internet anonymously and bypass geographic restrictions. This feature ensures secure access to content worldwide.

3. **Private Browsing Mode:**

- With private or incognito mode, users can browse without leaving a trace. This feature prevents the storage of cookies, browsing history, and cached files.

4. **Decentralized Identity (DID):**

- The browser supports decentralized identity protocols, enabling users to control their digital identities securely without relying on centralized authorities.

By putting privacy first, the Mises Browser empowers users to reclaim control over their online presence and reduce exposure to digital surveillance.

Ad and Tracker Blocking

Intrusive ads and trackers are among the most significant irritants of modern browsing. The Mises Browser tackles this issue head-on with powerful ad-blocking and anti-tracking capabilities.

1. **Comprehensive Ad Blocking:**

   o The browser automatically blocks ads across websites, ensuring an uninterrupted and clutter-free browsing experience. This feature also improves page load speeds and reduces data consumption.

2. **Tracker Detection and Blocking:**

   o Trackers embedded in websites monitor user behavior to build detailed profiles for targeted advertising. The Mises Browser identifies and blocks these trackers, safeguarding your privacy.

3. **Customizable Blocking Rules:**

   o Users can fine-tune the ad and tracker-blocking settings to meet their specific needs. For example,

you can whitelist certain websites
or enable advanced blocking for
heightened security.

4. **Anti-Fingerprinting Technology:**

   ○ Websites often use fingerprinting
   techniques to identify unique user
   profiles based on device and
   browser configurations. The Mises
   Browser employs
   anti-fingerprinting measures to
   make users less identifiable online.

By eliminating ads and trackers, the browser not
only protects user privacy but also enhances
usability and performance.

Enhanced Speed Optimization

Speed is a critical factor in providing a seamless
browsing experience. The Mises Browser
leverages advanced technologies to deliver

blazing-fast performance, even on resource-intensive websites.

1. **Efficient Resource Management:**

   ○ The browser optimizes CPU and RAM usage, ensuring smooth performance even with multiple tabs open. Its lightweight design minimizes strain on devices, making it ideal for older or low-spec hardware.

2. **Preloading Technology:**

   ○ Mises uses intelligent preloading to anticipate the user's next actions, loading content in advance to reduce delays. This feature is particularly effective on dynamic websites and web applications.

3. **Ad-Free Loading:**

   ○ By blocking ads and trackers, the browser reduces the amount of data that needs to be loaded, significantly speeding up webpage rendering times.

4. **Optimized for Web3:**

   ○ Blockchain interactions, such as connecting to dApps or conducting crypto transactions, are handled efficiently, minimizing delays commonly associated with decentralized networks.

With its focus on speed optimization, the Mises Browser ensures that users can browse, transact, and interact with content quickly and efficiently.

Decentralized Applications (dApps) Integration

The Mises Browser stands out for its seamless support of decentralized applications (dApps), making it an essential tool for users exploring the Web3 ecosystem.

1. **Native Blockchain Support:**

   - The browser provides out-of-the-box compatibility with major blockchain networks such as Ethereum, Binance Smart Chain, and Polygon. This allows users to interact with dApps directly without requiring additional plugins or extensions.

2. **Built-In Cryptocurrency Wallet:**

   - A secure, multi-chain cryptocurrency wallet is integrated into the browser, enabling users to:
     - Store, send, and receive cryptocurrencies.
     - Monitor real-time portfolio values.
     - Participate in decentralized finance (DeFi) activities like staking and lending.

3. **Seamless dApp Connectivity:**

- ○ With just a few clicks, users can connect their wallet to dApps, unlocking functionalities such as trading on decentralized exchanges, participating in blockchain-based games, and managing non-fungible tokens (NFTs).

4. **Cross-Chain Compatibility:**

- ○ The browser's cross-chain capabilities enable users to interact with multiple blockchain ecosystems from a single interface, streamlining the Web3 experience.

5. **dApp Marketplace:**

- ○ A curated dApp marketplace is accessible within the browser, showcasing popular and verified dApps across various categories, including finance, gaming, and social networking.

6. **Developer-Friendly Tools:**

o The browser includes tools for developers to test and deploy their own dApps, making it a valuable resource for blockchain innovators.

By integrating dApp functionality directly into its platform, the Mises Browser simplifies access to the decentralized web, empowering users to fully engage with the next generation of online applications.

Navigating the Interface

The Mises Browser offers a sleek, intuitive interface designed to enhance usability while accommodating advanced features. Its interface balances simplicity with functionality, making it equally accessible to novices and experienced users. In this section, we'll explore how to navigate the toolbar, customize your homepage, and manage bookmarks and tabs effectively.

Exploring the Toolbar

The toolbar is the Mises Browser's command center, giving users easy access to core functionalities. Understanding its layout and features is key to navigating efficiently.

1. **Address Bar and Search Functionality:**

   ○ **Unified Input Field:** The address
     bar doubles as a search bar,
     allowing users to enter URLs
     directly or search the web.
   ○ **Search Engine Integration:** Users
     can select from multiple search
     engines, including privacy-focused
     options like DuckDuckGo or
     decentralized search engines
     tailored to Web3.

2. **Navigation Controls:**

   ○ **Back and Forward Buttons:**
     Navigate to previously visited
     pages or move forward if you've
     returned to an earlier page.
   ○ **Refresh/Reload Button:** Quickly
     reload a page to view updated
     content.
   ○ **Home Button:** Instantly return to
     your customized homepage for

quick access to your most-used
resources.

3. **Extension and Plugin Access:**

   ○ The toolbar houses icons for
   installed extensions, such as ad
   blockers or cryptocurrency wallets,
   providing quick access to these
   tools.

4. **Menu Button:**

   ○ The menu button opens a dropdown
   panel offering access to settings,
   history, downloads, and developer
   tools.

5. **Privacy Controls:**

   ○ Features like private browsing
   mode, tracker blocking, and VPN
   toggles are conveniently placed on
   the toolbar for instant activation.

6. **dApp Connectivity Button:**

○ A dedicated icon enables seamless connection to decentralized applications, allowing users to interact with blockchain services with just one click.

Customizing Your Homepage

The homepage is the first thing users see when they open the Mises Browser, and customizing it ensures a tailored and efficient browsing experience.

1. **Setting Up Quick Access Links:**

   ○ Add shortcuts to your favorite websites, such as email, social media, or frequently used dApps.
   ○ Arrange shortcuts in a grid format for easy visibility and accessibility.

2. **Background Customization:**

o Choose from preloaded themes, upload your own background image, or opt for a minimalist solid color for a distraction-free environment.

3. **News and Feeds Integration:**

   o Enable news widgets or RSS feeds to display updates directly on your homepage. These can be tailored to specific interests, such as blockchain news or general topics.

4. **Search Engine Preferences:**

   o Set your preferred search engine to streamline search queries directly from the homepage.

5. **Widgets and Functional Panels:**

   o Add weather updates, calendar reminders, or crypto portfolio tracking widgets to your homepage for a more personalized experience.

6. Privacy Settings for the Homepage:

- Disable cookies or tracking elements for a secure and private browsing experience, even on the homepage.

Customizing your homepage not only makes it visually appealing but also transforms it into a productivity hub tailored to your needs.

Managing Bookmarks and Tabs

Efficient management of bookmarks and tabs is crucial for streamlined browsing, especially for users juggling multiple tasks or exploring various dApps.

1. Bookmarks Management:

- **Creating Bookmarks:** Save frequently visited pages by clicking the star icon in the address bar.

Organize them into folders for better categorization.

- ○ **Bookmark Bar:** Enable the bookmark bar to display your most-used links below the toolbar for quick access.
- ○ **Importing and Exporting Bookmarks:** Mises Browser allows you to import bookmarks from other browsers or export your collection for backup.
- ○ **Bookmark Search:** Quickly locate specific bookmarks using the search functionality in the bookmark manager.

2. **Tab Management:**

- ○ **Multiple Tabs:** Open numerous tabs without sacrificing performance, thanks to the browser's efficient resource management.
- ○ **Tab Groups:** Organize tabs into groups based on tasks, topics, or

categories. This feature is particularly useful for researchers and multitaskers.

- ○ **Pinning Tabs:** Keep essential tabs, such as email or task managers, always accessible by pinning them to the left of the tab bar.
- ○ **Tab Previews:** Hover over a tab to view a small preview of its content, making it easier to identify the tab you need.
- ○ **Session Restore:** Automatically restore tabs from your last session if the browser is accidentally closed or crashes.

3. **Advanced Features:**

- ○ **Vertical Tabs:** Switch to a vertical tab layout for better organization, especially on widescreen monitors.
- ○ **Tab Snoozing:** Temporarily "snooze" unused tabs to save system resources and reopen them later.

○ **Private Tabs:** Open tabs in private browsing mode alongside regular tabs for simultaneous secure and standard browsing.

4. **Cloud Syncing:**

○ Sync your bookmarks and tabs across multiple devices using the browser's cloud integration feature. This ensures a seamless browsing experience, whether on a desktop, tablet, or mobile device.

Privacy and Security Features in Mises Browser

Privacy and security are foundational pillars of the Mises Browser, making it a standout choice for users who prioritize digital safety. With cutting-edge technologies, robust encryption methods, and user-friendly tools, the browser ensures that your data remains private while providing secure interactions across the web.

Advanced Encryption Options

Encryption is a vital mechanism for protecting sensitive information. The Mises Browser employs state-of-the-art encryption protocols to safeguard your online activities, ensuring that malicious actors cannot intercept your data.

1. **End-to-End Encryption:**

   o The browser utilizes end-to-end encryption (E2EE) for features such as private messaging, file transfers, and interactions with decentralized applications (dApps). This ensures that only you and the intended recipient can access the shared information.

2. **Secure HTTPS Connections:**

   o By default, the Mises Browser prioritizes secure HTTPS connections over less secure HTTP. The integrated HTTPS enforcement prevents unsecured connections and alerts users when a website lacks proper encryption.

3. **Encrypted DNS Requests:**

   ○ Mises Browser supports DNS-over-HTTPS (DoH) and DNS-over-TLS (DoT) protocols, encrypting your DNS queries to prevent third-party interception or tampering. This feature protects your browsing history from being monitored by ISPs or hackers.

4. **Data Encryption for Cloud Syncing:**

   ○ Any data synchronized across devices, such as bookmarks or session information, is encrypted using advanced cryptographic algorithms. This ensures that even if the data is intercepted, it remains indecipherable.

5. **Password Manager with Encryption:**

o The built-in password manager securely stores your credentials using AES-256 encryption, the industry standard for protecting sensitive data. This eliminates the need to remember multiple passwords while keeping your accounts secure.

Secure Wallet Management

For users interacting with blockchain technologies and cryptocurrencies, the Mises Browser offers a secure wallet management system.

1. **Built-In Wallet Integration:**

   o The browser includes a native cryptocurrency wallet, enabling you to store, send, and receive various digital assets securely.

- Private keys and seed phrases are stored locally on your device rather than on centralized servers, significantly reducing the risk of hacking.

2. **Multi-Layer Authentication:**

- Wallet access is protected by multi-layer authentication options, including PIN codes, biometric verification (such as fingerprints or facial recognition), and two-factor authentication (2FA).

3. **Transaction Verification:**

- Every transaction requires explicit user approval. The browser provides detailed transaction information, including gas fees and recipient addresses, to prevent accidental or malicious transfers.

4. **Cold Wallet Connectivity:**

○ The Mises Browser supports hardware wallets, allowing you to connect your cold wallet devices for an additional layer of security during transactions.

5. **Anti-Phishing Protection:**

○ Integrated anti-phishing features help identify and block fraudulent websites that attempt to steal your wallet credentials or assets.

Using VPN and Proxy Settings

To ensure comprehensive online anonymity and security, the Mises Browser integrates robust VPN and proxy settings.

1. **Built-In VPN Integration:**

○ The browser features a built-in VPN service that encrypts your internet connection, masking your

IP address and protecting your data from prying eyes.

○ Users can select servers from multiple regions, enabling access to geo-restricted content while maintaining privacy.

2. **Custom Proxy Configuration:**

○ For advanced users, the browser allows custom proxy settings, including HTTP, HTTPS, and SOCKS5 proxies. This flexibility is ideal for those needing to route their traffic through specific servers for additional privacy or to bypass restrictions.

3. **Kill Switch Feature:**

○ The VPN includes a kill switch that automatically disconnects your internet connection if the VPN service is interrupted. This ensures your real IP address is never exposed, even temporarily.

4. No-Logs Policy:

- The built-in VPN adheres to a strict no-logs policy, ensuring that none of your browsing activity or connection details are stored or shared.

5. Split Tunneling:

- The VPN supports split tunneling, allowing you to route certain applications or websites outside the VPN while securing the rest of your traffic.

6. DNS Leak Protection:

- Advanced DNS leak protection ensures that no data leaks outside the encrypted VPN tunnel, maintaining your anonymity.

How These Features Work Together

The combination of advanced encryption, secure wallet management, and robust VPN/proxy options creates a cohesive security ecosystem within the Mises Browser. Here's how these features enhance your online experience:

- **Data Privacy:** Encryption and VPN settings ensure your data is hidden from unauthorized access, even on public Wi-Fi networks.
- **Financial Security:** The secure wallet integration safeguards your digital assets from theft, phishing, and hacking attempts.
- **Anonymity:** VPN and proxy options mask your identity and location, making it difficult for websites or third parties to track you.

Built-In Cryptocurrency Wallet

The Mises Browser sets itself apart with an integrated cryptocurrency wallet, designed for seamless interaction with blockchain networks and digital assets. Whether you're a seasoned crypto trader or a novice exploring decentralized finance (DeFi), the wallet provides robust functionality, strong security, and user-friendly features.

Setting Up Your Wallet

Setting up the built-in cryptocurrency wallet is a straightforward process, even for beginners. The browser guides you step-by-step, ensuring that your wallet is ready to use in minutes.

1. **Accessing the Wallet:**

   ○ Navigate to the toolbar and locate the wallet icon. Clicking on it opens the wallet interface.
   ○ New users will be prompted to set up their wallet or import an existing one.

2. **Creating a New Wallet:**

   ○ Select "Create New Wallet" and follow the prompts to generate a wallet.
   ○ You'll receive a unique seed phrase (typically 12 or 24 words) during the setup process.
       ■ **Important:** Write down your seed phrase and store it securely offline. Losing it means losing access to your funds.

- ○ Set a strong password for additional protection.

3. **Importing an Existing Wallet:**

   - ○ Choose "Import Wallet" if you already have a cryptocurrency wallet.
   - ○ Enter the seed phrase or private key from your existing wallet to import your account seamlessly.

4. **Connecting to Networks:**

   - ○ The wallet supports multiple blockchain networks. Select the desired network, such as Ethereum, Binance Smart Chain, or others, depending on your use case.

5. **Customization Options:**

   - ○ Personalize your wallet by setting display preferences, such as default currency (e.g., USD, EUR) and transaction notifications.

Supported Cryptocurrencies

The built-in wallet supports a wide array of cryptocurrencies, catering to diverse user needs:

1. **Major Cryptocurrencies:**

   - Bitcoin (BTC)
   - Ethereum (ETH)
   - Binance Coin (BNB)

2. **Stablecoins:**

   - Tether (USDT)
   - USD Coin (USDC)
   - Dai (DAI)

3. **Tokens:**

   - ERC-20 tokens on the Ethereum network.
   - BEP-20 tokens on Binance Smart Chain.

4. **dApps and NFTs:**

- o The wallet integrates with decentralized applications (dApps), allowing users to interact with DeFi protocols and purchase or store NFTs (non-fungible tokens).

5. **Future Support:**

- o Regular updates add support for emerging cryptocurrencies and new blockchain ecosystems, ensuring compatibility with the latest technologies.

Sending and Receiving Payments

The wallet streamlines cryptocurrency transactions with an intuitive interface, making it easy to send and receive payments.

1. **Sending Payments:**

- o Open the wallet and select the "Send" option.

- Enter the recipient's wallet address. Double-check the address to avoid errors.
- Specify the amount to send, and choose the cryptocurrency or token.
- Review transaction details, including gas fees, before confirming the transaction.
- Confirm the transaction using your password, PIN, or biometric authentication.

2. **Receiving Payments:**

- Select the "Receive" option in the wallet.
- Copy your wallet address or scan the QR code provided.
- Share the address or QR code with the sender.
- Monitor your wallet for incoming funds. Once the transaction is confirmed on the blockchain, your balance will update.

3. **Transaction History:**

   o The wallet maintains a detailed
   transaction history, showing sent
   and received payments, gas fees,
   and timestamps.

4. **Cross-Chain Transfers:**

   o If supported, you can transfer assets
   between different blockchain
   networks using built-in bridges or
   third-party integrations.

Security Best Practices for Wallet Use

Cryptocurrency wallets handle sensitive
financial data, making security paramount. The
Mises Browser offers built-in safeguards, but
users should also follow these best practices:

1. **Secure Your Seed Phrase:**

○ Write down your seed phrase on paper and store it in a safe place. Avoid saving it digitally, as it may be vulnerable to hacking.

2. **Use Strong Passwords:**

○ Choose a password that combines uppercase and lowercase letters, numbers, and special characters. Avoid using easily guessable information.

3. **Enable Biometric Authentication:**

○ Use fingerprint or facial recognition, if available, to add an extra layer of security.

4. **Regular Updates:**

○ Keep your browser and wallet software updated to protect against known vulnerabilities.

5. **Beware of Phishing Attempts:**

○ Only interact with trusted dApps and websites. Avoid clicking on suspicious links or providing wallet information to unverified sources.

6. **Two-Factor Authentication (2FA):**

○ Enable 2FA wherever possible, especially when interacting with third-party services linked to your wallet.

7. **Cold Wallets for Large Holdings:**

○ For substantial crypto holdings, consider transferring funds to a cold wallet (offline hardware wallet) to minimize exposure to online risks.

8. **Monitor Transactions:**

○ Regularly review your wallet activity for unauthorized transactions. Report any suspicious activity immediately.

Web3 and Decentralized Applications (dApps)

The digital world is evolving rapidly, and the advent of **Web3** and **Decentralized Applications (dApps)** marks a transformative shift in how users interact with the internet. Web3 represents a decentralized, blockchain-based iteration of the web, giving users more control over their data, assets, and interactions. At the heart of this revolution are dApps, which enable trustless and permissionless interactions.

Introduction to Web3

Web3, often called the "decentralized web," is a paradigm shift from Web2, the current iteration dominated by centralized platforms. It leverages blockchain technology to decentralize data storage, decision-making, and ownership. Unlike traditional systems, Web3 empowers users by giving them direct control over their digital presence.

Key Features of Web3:

1. **Decentralization:** Unlike Web2, where servers and databases are controlled by companies, Web3 relies on decentralized networks. Data is distributed across blockchain nodes, eliminating single points of failure.
2. **Ownership and Control:** Web3 provides users with ownership of their data, digital assets, and identities through wallets and private keys.

3. **Transparency:** Blockchain-based transactions are public and immutable, fostering trust and reducing fraud.

4. **Tokenization:** Cryptocurrencies and tokens fuel Web3 economies, enabling microtransactions, staking, and incentivization mechanisms.

5. **Smart Contracts:** Self-executing contracts on blockchains facilitate secure and automated interactions between parties.

Real-World Applications of Web3:

- **DeFi (Decentralized Finance):** Enabling financial services like lending, borrowing, and trading without intermediaries.
- **NFTs (Non-Fungible Tokens):** Allowing users to tokenize digital art, collectibles, and intellectual property.
- **Gaming:** Powering play-to-earn models and digital asset ownership.
- **Supply Chain:** Enhancing traceability and accountability.

Accessing and Using dApps

Decentralized applications, or **dApps**, are Web3's cornerstone. Unlike traditional apps, dApps operate on decentralized networks, often using smart contracts to perform their functions.

How dApps Differ from Traditional Apps:

1. **Backend on Blockchain:** While traditional apps run on centralized servers, dApps use blockchain as their backend.
2. **Trustless Interaction:** Users interact directly with the blockchain, reducing reliance on intermediaries.
3. **Token Utilization:** Many dApps incorporate tokens for payments, governance, or utility.

Accessing dApps:

1. **Using a Web3 Browser:**

    ○ Browsers like the Mises Browser have built-in Web3 capabilities, allowing seamless access to dApps.

    ○ Simply navigate to the desired dApp's URL or use the browser's dApp marketplace to explore available options.

2. **Connecting a Wallet:**

    ○ Most dApps require you to connect a cryptocurrency wallet, such as MetaMask, Trust Wallet, or the Mises integrated wallet.

    ○ Grant permissions carefully to avoid scams.

3. **Navigating the Interface:**

    ○ Once connected, dApps provide interfaces for various actions, like swapping tokens, staking assets, or playing games.

    ○ Transactions often require blockchain confirmation, incurring gas fees.

Popular Categories of dApps:

- **Finance:** Examples include Uniswap (decentralized exchange) and Aave (lending platform).
- **Gaming:** Axie Infinity and Decentraland combine gaming with digital asset ownership.
- **Social Media:** Lens Protocol and Mastodon prioritize user-controlled data and censorship-free interactions.
- **Marketplaces:** OpenSea allows users to trade NFTs securely.

Best Practices for Using dApps:

1. Verify the dApp's authenticity and security credentials.
2. Read reviews and community feedback before engaging with a new dApp.
3. Start with small transactions to minimize risk while learning the platform.

Integrating with Blockchain Networks

Integration with blockchain networks is a fundamental aspect of Web3. Blockchain enables the transparency, security, and decentralization that dApps and Web3 services rely on.

What is Blockchain Integration? Integration refers to the ability of a dApp or Web3 service to interact with one or more blockchain networks. This interaction is essential for executing smart contracts, processing transactions, and managing assets.

Steps to Integrate with Blockchain Networks:

1. **Choose the Blockchain:**
   - Popular options include Ethereum, Binance Smart Chain, Polygon, and Solana. Each offers unique features like scalability, speed, or low transaction costs.
   - Consider the dApp's requirements, such as smart contract functionality, token standards, or developer tools.
2. **Connect a Wallet:**

- ○ Wallets act as gateways between users and blockchains. Integration requires users to connect their wallets to interact with dApps.

3. **Smart Contract Deployment:**
   - ○ Developers create smart contracts to define the rules of interaction on the blockchain. Users interact with these contracts through dApps.

4. **Enable Cross-Chain Capabilities:**
   - ○ Some dApps support cross-chain interactions, allowing users to transfer assets or data between different blockchains. This may involve using bridges or multi-chain platforms.

Popular Blockchain Networks and Their Features:

1. **Ethereum (ETH):**
   - ○ The most widely used blockchain for dApps and smart contracts. Supports ERC-20 tokens and DeFi protocols.

- Pros: Robust developer community, high decentralization.
  - **Cons:** High gas fees and slower transaction times.
2. **Binance Smart Chain (BSC):**
   - Known for low transaction fees and faster confirmations.
   - Ideal for DeFi and gaming dApps.
3. **Polygon (MATIC):**
   - A Layer 2 solution for Ethereum, offering scalability and cost efficiency.
4. **Solana (SOL):**
   - High-speed transactions with low fees. Suitable for gaming and high-frequency applications.

The Future of Web3 and dApps

As Web3 continues to evolve, dApps are becoming more sophisticated, accessible, and integral to our digital experiences. Innovations in scalability, user experience, and security are addressing early limitations, paving the way for widespread adoption. Future developments may include:

- **Enhanced Interoperability:** Improved cross-chain integration for seamless interactions across blockchains.
- **User-Friendly Interfaces:** Simplified onboarding and navigation for non-technical users.
- **Increased Decentralization:** A broader shift from Web2 to Web3 principles in everyday applications.

Customization and Extensions in the Mises Browser

One of the defining features of the Mises Browser is its high degree of customizability. By allowing users to personalize their browsing experience and add functionality through extensions, the browser adapts seamlessly to individual preferences. From productivity enhancements to aesthetic adjustments, users can craft a browsing environment tailored to their needs.

Installing and Managing Extensions

Extensions are small software add-ons that enhance the functionality of the Mises Browser. These tools enable users to incorporate additional features such as ad blockers, password managers, note-taking apps, and more.

1. Accessing the Extensions Library:

- Open the browser's **Settings Menu** and navigate to the **Extensions** section.
- The Mises Browser provides access to a built-in library of extensions compatible with the browser.
- Alternatively, users can install extensions from third-party marketplaces, provided they are Web3-friendly and secure.

2. Installing Extensions:

- **Step 1:** Browse the available extensions in the library.
- **Step 2:** Select an extension by clicking on it to view details such as features, reviews, and permissions.

- **Step 3:** Click the **Install** button. Follow any on-screen instructions to complete the installation.
- **Step 4:** Once installed, the extension icon will appear on the browser toolbar for quick access.

3. Managing Extensions:

- **Enabling/Disabling:** Go to the **Extensions** section in settings to toggle extensions on or off without uninstalling them.
- **Updating:** Regular updates ensure compatibility and security. Use the **Update All Extensions** button in the settings menu to check for and apply updates.
- **Uninstalling:** Remove extensions no longer needed by selecting the extension and clicking **Uninstall**.
- **Permissions Management:** Review and modify the permissions granted to each extension for better privacy and security.

4. Best Practices for Managing Extensions:

- Only install extensions from trusted sources to minimize the risk of malware.
- Regularly review installed extensions and remove those no longer in use.
- Monitor browser performance, as too many extensions can slow down loading times.

Optimizing for Productivity

The Mises Browser provides a range of features and customizations to help users stay organized and focused while browsing. By tailoring settings and using productivity-centric extensions, you can create a distraction-free browsing environment.

1. Productivity-Focused Extensions:

- **Task Management Tools:** Integrate apps like Todoist or Asana to keep track of tasks and deadlines directly in the browser.

- **Note-Taking Extensions:** Use tools such as Evernote Web Clipper or Notion to save and organize research and ideas.
- **Focus and Time Management Tools:** Add extensions like StayFocusd or LeechBlock to block distracting websites during work hours.
- **File Management Integrations:** Sync with cloud services like Google Drive or Dropbox to access files quickly.

2. Built-In Productivity Features:

- **Tab Management:** Utilize features like tab grouping and pinning to organize open tabs. Close inactive tabs to free up system resources.
- **Bookmark Organization:** Create folders for bookmarks to categorize frequently visited sites.
- **Reading Mode:** Activate this mode for a clutter-free reading experience by

removing ads and unnecessary formatting from articles.

3. Custom Keyboard Shortcuts:

- Configure shortcuts in the browser settings to streamline repetitive actions, such as opening new tabs, bookmarking pages, or switching between tabs.

4. Sync Across Devices:

- Enable the synchronization feature to access bookmarks, settings, and extensions across multiple devices. This is especially useful for users who frequently switch between a desktop and mobile device.

Themes and Appearance Settings

Customizing the look and feel of your browser is more than just an aesthetic choice—it can enhance usability and comfort during long browsing sessions.

1. Changing Themes:

- The Mises Browser supports various themes, including light, dark, and high-contrast modes.
- To apply a theme:
    - Navigate to **Settings > Appearance > Themes**.
    - Browse the available options and select your preferred theme.
    - Some themes may adjust dynamically based on the time of day (e.g., switching to dark mode at night).

2. Creating a Personalized Look:

- **Custom Backgrounds:** Upload a personal image or select from a gallery of wallpapers to set as your homepage background.

- **Accent Colors:** Adjust the browser's accent color to match your preferences or branding.
- **Font Customization:** Modify font styles and sizes to improve readability.

3. Toolbar Customization:

- Rearrange toolbar icons for quick access to frequently used features.
- Add or remove buttons from the toolbar, such as bookmarks, history, or extensions, depending on your needs.

4. Accessibility Features:

- **High-Contrast Mode:** Enhance visibility for users with visual impairments by increasing color contrast.
- **Zoom Settings:** Set a default zoom level for all websites or use per-site zoom adjustments.
- **Reader-Friendly Fonts:** Enable fonts designed for dyslexia or other reading challenges.

5. Dynamic Themes:

- Explore themes that change based on weather, time, or other real-time factors for an interactive browsing experience.

Troubleshooting and FAQs for the Mises Browser

Like any advanced software, the Mises Browser may occasionally encounter issues. This guide will help you troubleshoot common problems, report bugs effectively, and access support resources to resolve any challenges quickly and efficiently.

Common Issues and Solutions

Here are some frequently encountered problems and their solutions:

---

1. Slow Browsing Speed

Symptoms:

- Pages load slowly or fail to load entirely.
- Videos buffer excessively despite a stable internet connection.

Possible Causes:

- Too many open tabs consuming system resources.
- Outdated browser version.
- Extensions interfering with performance.

Solutions:

- Close unnecessary tabs and restart the browser.
- Check for and install updates by navigating to **Settings > About Mises Browser**.
- Disable or uninstall extensions that may be causing conflicts.

- Clear browser cache under **Settings > Privacy and Security > Clear Browsing Data**.

---

2. Extension Compatibility Issues

Symptoms:

- Extensions fail to work or crash the browser.
- New extensions won't install.

Possible Causes:

- Using incompatible or outdated extensions.
- Insufficient permissions for the extension.

Solutions:

- Verify the extension's compatibility with the Mises Browser by checking the extension details.
- Update the extension from the extension manager.

- Grant required permissions under **Settings > Extensions**.
- If the problem persists, uninstall and reinstall the extension.

---

3. Issues with Built-In Cryptocurrency Wallet

Symptoms:

- Unable to set up or access the wallet.
- Errors when sending or receiving payments.

Possible Causes:

- Incorrect wallet setup.
- Network connectivity issues with the blockchain.

Solutions:

- Recheck wallet setup by following the steps in **Settings > Wallet > Setup**.
- Ensure the browser is connected to a stable internet connection.

- Switch to a different blockchain node under **Settings > Wallet > Network Options**.
- Contact support if funds appear lost or inaccessible.

---

4. Frequent Browser Crashes

Symptoms:

- Browser closes unexpectedly during use.
- Errors during startup.

Possible Causes:

- Corrupted installation files.
- Conflicts with third-party software or extensions.

Solutions:

- Restart your device and reopen the browser.
- Reinstall the browser by downloading the latest version from the official website.

- Temporarily disable extensions to identify if one is causing the issue.

---

5. Difficulty Accessing Decentralized Applications (dApps)

Symptoms:

- Unable to connect to dApps.
- Transactions fail or timeout.

Possible Causes:

- Outdated blockchain integration settings.
- Connectivity issues with the dApp server.

Solutions:

- Update your blockchain settings under **Settings > Web3**.
- Check the dApp's server status on its official website.
- Clear browser cookies and cache for the specific dApp.

How to Report Bugs

When encountering issues that can't be resolved with troubleshooting, reporting the bug ensures that developers can address the problem promptly. Follow these steps to report a bug effectively:

1. Collect Information:

- Describe the issue in detail, including steps to reproduce it.
- Note your operating system, browser version, and any error messages.
- Include screenshots or screen recordings to demonstrate the issue.

2. Submit a Bug Report:

- Go to the **Support** section in the browser's settings or visit the official Mises Browser website.
- Navigate to the **Report a Bug** page.

- Fill out the bug report form, providing all relevant information and attachments.
- Submit the report and await a response from the support team.

3. Follow Up:

- If you don't receive a timely response, check the status of your report through the support portal.
- Provide additional information if requested by the support team.

Tips for Effective Bug Reporting:

- Be concise but thorough. Include only relevant details to help developers pinpoint the issue.
- Use clear, descriptive titles for your bug reports (e.g., "Browser Crashes When Accessing Wallet").
- Test the problem on different devices or networks, if possible, to identify patterns.

Accessing Support

The Mises Browser provides multiple support channels to help users resolve issues quickly:

---

1. In-App Help Center:

- Access the **Help Center** through the browser's settings menu.
- Browse an extensive library of articles, FAQs, and troubleshooting guides for common problems.

---

2. Community Forums:

- Join the Mises Browser community forums to connect with other users and find solutions.
- Participate in discussions to share tips and get advice from experienced users.
- Forums are also a great place to learn about updates and feature requests.

3. Live Chat Support:

- Some versions of the Mises Browser include a live chat option under **Support > Contact Us**.
- Speak directly with a support agent for immediate assistance.

4. Email Support:

- Email the support team at **support@misesbrowser.com**.
- Include a detailed description of the issue and any relevant files or screenshots.

5. Social Media and Updates:

- Follow the Mises Browser on platforms like Twitter or Discord for announcements and support.

- Engage with the development team and stay updated on upcoming features and fixes.

---

6. Feedback Submission:

- Share your thoughts or suggestions by using the **Feedback** feature in the settings menu.
- User feedback plays a critical role in improving the browser's functionality.

Advanced Features for Power Users in the Mises Browser

The Mises Browser is not only a tool for everyday browsing but also a robust platform designed for power users who demand advanced functionality. Whether you're a developer, a blockchain enthusiast, or someone seeking granular control over privacy, the browser has features tailored to your needs. Below, we explore its advanced capabilities.

Developer Tools Overview

Developer tools are essential for web developers and tech enthusiasts who need to debug, inspect, and optimize web applications. The Mises Browser includes a sophisticated set of developer tools that rival those of leading browsers.

---

1. Inspect Element and DOM Manipulation

- **Inspect Element** allows you to view and edit HTML and CSS in real-time. Right-click on any element on a webpage and select **Inspect** to access the DOM structure.
- Modify elements on-the-fly to test design changes or troubleshoot layout issues.

Key Features:

- Real-time CSS editing with instant visual feedback.
- Highlighting of CSS box models for better understanding of margins, padding, and borders.

- View dynamically generated content for JavaScript-heavy pages.

---

2. JavaScript Console

- The **Console** tab provides an environment to test, debug, and execute JavaScript code.
- Use it to log data, debug scripts, or interact with Web3 APIs and smart contracts.

Key Features:

- Execute custom JavaScript commands.
- Debug errors with stack traces and error messages.
- Access detailed logs from Web3 interactions.

---

3. Network Monitoring

- The **Network** tab lets you monitor and analyze all HTTP/HTTPS requests and responses made by a webpage.
- Useful for debugging API requests, optimizing page load times, or troubleshooting connectivity issues.

Key Features:

- Inspect request headers, response data, and timings.
- Analyze WebSocket connections and real-time data exchanges.
- View and debug blockchain API calls for dApp interactions.

---

4. Performance Profiling

- Optimize your applications by identifying bottlenecks in your code with the **Performance** tab.
- Record and analyze the runtime of scripts, rendering, and other processes.

Key Features:

- Frame-by-frame analysis of page rendering.
- Insights into memory usage and garbage collection.
- Evaluate Web3 transactions and blockchain integration performance.

---

5. Security and Lighthouse Audits

- Perform security checks on websites to identify vulnerabilities.
- Use Lighthouse to evaluate page performance, accessibility, and best practices.

Key Features:

- Audit dApps for compliance with blockchain security standards.
- Generate detailed reports to improve your app's performance and security.

Running Node.js Applications

The Mises Browser supports running **Node.js applications**, a feature that empowers developers to test and deploy server-side applications directly within the browser.

1. Setting Up Node.js in the Browser

- Download and install the Node.js runtime from the Mises Browser's plugin repository.
- Navigate to **Settings > Developer Tools > Enable Node.js** to activate support.

2. Testing Smart Contracts

- Power users working with blockchain technology can deploy and test smart contracts directly within the browser using Node.js.

- Integrate libraries like **Web3.js** or **Ethers.js** for seamless interaction with blockchain networks.

---

3. Running Scripts

- Open the developer console and use Node.js commands to execute server-side scripts or interact with APIs.
- Example: Run a blockchain transaction script to test Web3 compatibility.

Sample Code Snippet:

const Web3 = require('web3');

const web3 = new Web3('https://mainnet.infura.io/v3/YOUR-PROJECT-ID');

// Check the balance of an Ethereum address

web3.eth.getBalance('0xYourEthereumAddress')

```
.then(balance =>
console.log(web3.utils.fromWei(balance,
'ether')));
```

---

4. Benefits of Running Node.js Applications

- Local testing environment for blockchain and decentralized applications.
- Reduced need for external development environments.
- Integrated debugging and logging tools.

Advanced Privacy Settings

The Mises Browser offers unparalleled privacy controls, enabling users to customize their online footprint.

---

1. Custom Privacy Modes

- In addition to standard incognito browsing, the browser supports customizable privacy modes.
- Users can configure settings to disable cookies, trackers, and even JavaScript for specific sites.

Steps to Enable Custom Privacy Modes:

1. Navigate to **Settings > Privacy and Security**.
2. Select **Custom Privacy Mode** and define site-specific rules.
3. Save configurations and activate them when needed.

---

2. Granular Permission Controls

- Control how websites access sensitive information such as location, camera, microphone, and clipboard.
- Enable permissions on a per-site basis.

How to Manage Permissions:

1. Go to **Settings > Site Settings**.
2. Customize permissions for each website.

---

3. Advanced Tracker Blocking

- Beyond standard ad-blocking, the browser can block fingerprinting scripts, cryptocurrency mining scripts, and advanced trackers.
- Powered by AI-driven databases, the browser updates its tracker definitions regularly.

---

4. Enhanced Encryption Options

- Use advanced encryption settings to protect sensitive data during browsing sessions.
- Configure end-to-end encryption for browser-to-server communications.

---

5. VPN and Proxy Integration

- Enhance privacy further by routing your internet traffic through a VPN or proxy directly within the browser.
- Built-in options include toggling VPN/proxy on and off without requiring third-party software.

Mises Browser Ecosystem

The Mises Browser is more than just a tool for decentralized browsing; it represents a robust ecosystem driven by its community, developers, and commitment to innovation. Its ecosystem thrives on collaboration, regular updates, and a forward-looking vision for the future of Web3 and privacy-centric browsing.

Community and Developer Support

One of the strongest aspects of the Mises Browser is its vibrant community and dedicated developer network. The browser fosters an environment where users and developers can actively participate in shaping its features and improvements.

1. Engaged User Community

The Mises Browser community spans privacy enthusiasts, Web3 advocates, developers, and blockchain users.

- **Forums and Discussion Boards**: Users can join forums like Reddit, Discord, and Telegram to share feedback, seek solutions, and exchange tips.
- **Social Media Presence**: The Mises team maintains active profiles on Twitter, LinkedIn, and YouTube to provide updates and engage with the user base.
- **User-Centric Focus**: Regular surveys and beta testing programs allow users to influence feature development and priority fixes.

2. Dedicated Developer Support

Developers form the backbone of the Mises ecosystem, driving innovations and ensuring stability.

- **Developer Documentation**: Comprehensive documentation is available to guide developers in building, debugging, and deploying decentralized applications (dApps) for the browser.
- **API Access**: The browser offers APIs for developers to integrate custom tools and features seamlessly into the ecosystem.
- **Bug Bounty Programs**: Developers are incentivized to identify and report vulnerabilities through bug bounty initiatives, ensuring robust security.

3. Educational Resources

The browser ecosystem includes learning resources such as tutorials, webinars, and knowledge bases to support both novice and experienced users.

- Video guides and FAQs simplify the onboarding process for new users.
- Developers benefit from code examples, SDKs, and step-by-step integration guides.

Updates and Future Developments

The Mises Browser is a dynamic platform that evolves with the rapid pace of Web3 and blockchain technology. Regular updates ensure users have access to cutting-edge features and a seamless browsing experience.

1. Frequent Updates

- **Feature Enhancements**: Updates introduce new features, improve existing tools, and optimize performance.
- **Security Patches**: Regular security updates address vulnerabilities and implement the latest cryptographic standards.

- **User Feedback Integration**:
  Feedback-driven updates prioritize
  user-requested features and functionality.

2. Roadmap for Future Development

The Mises Browser team actively shares its
development roadmap, providing users and
developers with a clear vision of the platform's
direction.

- **Planned Innovations**:
  - Advanced AI-driven privacy tools
    to detect and block emerging
    threats.
  - Expanded blockchain integrations
    for compatibility with new
    networks.
  - Enhanced Web3 dApp interfaces for
    seamless user experiences.
- **Decentralized Storage Integration**:
  Future updates aim to incorporate
  decentralized storage systems like IPFS
  (InterPlanetary File System), allowing

users to access and store data without reliance on centralized servers.

- **Cross-Platform Synchronization**: Plans to improve device synchronization for bookmarks, wallets, and preferences.

3. Scalability and Performance Improvements

- The development team is focused on optimizing browser performance to handle increasing demands from dApps and blockchain networks.
- Future updates will further reduce resource usage, ensuring smooth browsing even on lower-spec devices.

Contributing to Open Source

The Mises Browser is an open-source project, inviting users and developers to actively contribute to its growth and refinement. Open-source development not only fosters transparency but also encourages innovation through collective expertise.

1. Why Contribute?

- **Collaborative Innovation**: Developers can bring fresh ideas and unique perspectives to enhance the browser.
- **Community Recognition**: Contributors gain acknowledgment within the Web3 and open-source community.
- **Skill Development**: Working on cutting-edge technologies like blockchain and Web3 provides valuable experience.

2. How to Get Involved

- **Code Contributions**: Developers can contribute by fixing bugs, adding features, or optimizing existing code.
  - Visit the browser's GitHub repository to access the source code and identify open issues.
  - Submit pull requests for review and approval.
- **Documentation and Tutorials**: Non-developers can contribute by creating

or improving user guides, FAQs, and
tutorials.
- **Translations**: Help make the browser
  accessible to a global audience by
  translating it into different languages.
- **Testing**: Participate in beta testing
  programs to identify bugs and provide
  feedback on new features.

3. Governance and Collaboration

- **Open Governance Model**: Key decisions
  about the browser's direction are made
  transparently, with input from the
  community.
- **Collaborative Platforms**: Tools like
  GitHub, Discord, and collaborative wikis
  streamline communication and project
  management.

4. Supporting Through Donations

- Users who may not contribute code can
  support the project through financial
  donations.

- Cryptocurrency donations are accepted, reinforcing the browser's commitment to blockchain technology.

Case Studies and Use Cases

The Mises Browser has carved a niche for itself in the rapidly evolving landscape of decentralized technology, offering solutions that cater to privacy-conscious individuals, Web3 enthusiasts, and professionals navigating the blockchain ecosystem.

Real-World Applications of Mises Browser

The Mises Browser has been employed in diverse settings, from personal use to business environments. Its unique features address challenges in privacy, blockchain integration, and Web3 adoption. Below are some prominent applications:

1. Privacy-Conscious Browsing for Individuals

- **Scenario**: A journalist working in a country with strict internet censorship needed a secure way to access global news sources and communicate with whistleblowers.
- **Solution**: Using the Mises Browser's advanced encryption options and integrated VPN, the journalist bypassed geo-restrictions while maintaining anonymity.
- **Impact**: The browser enabled safe and unrestricted reporting, protecting the journalist's identity and preserving the integrity of their work.

2. Seamless Web3 Access for Developers

- **Scenario**: A blockchain developer required a browser optimized for testing decentralized applications (dApps) without delays or third-party vulnerabilities.

- **Solution**: The Mises Browser's dApp integration allowed the developer to interact directly with smart contracts and blockchain networks.
- **Impact**: The streamlined testing environment accelerated development timelines and improved the quality of their dApp projects.

3. Cryptocurrency Management for Freelancers

- **Scenario**: A freelance graphic designer accepting payments in cryptocurrencies faced challenges managing multiple wallets and transactions securely.
- **Solution**: The Mises Browser's built-in cryptocurrency wallet supported various coins, simplifying payment processing.
- **Impact**: With one secure platform for transactions, the designer reduced

operational inefficiencies and gained peace of mind regarding wallet security.

4. Enterprise Blockchain Adoption

- **Scenario**: A mid-sized logistics company sought a secure browser to integrate blockchain-based tracking systems into their operations.
- **Solution**: The Mises Browser facilitated access to enterprise-grade blockchain applications for real-time shipment tracking and data sharing.
- **Impact**: Improved transparency and reduced fraud across the supply chain boosted client trust and operational efficiency.

5. Academic Research and Collaboration

- **Scenario**: A university research team studying the effects of blockchain on global economics needed a secure, decentralized platform for data analysis and collaboration.

- **Solution**: By leveraging the browser's privacy-centric tools and Web3 integrations, the team accessed decentralized resources and maintained data confidentiality.
- **Impact**: The browser provided a collaborative and secure environment, enabling groundbreaking research and data sharing across borders.

Success Stories from Users

The Mises Browser's impact is best illustrated by the success stories of its users. Below are testimonials that demonstrate its value in real-world scenarios:

1. A Startup's Journey to Decentralized Success

- **User**: Blockchain startup founder in Silicon Valley
- **Challenge**: "We struggled to find a browser that supported the functionality

we needed for decentralized applications. Most mainstream browsers were too slow or didn't prioritize Web3 features."

- **Solution**: "With Mises Browser, we not only accessed dApps efficiently but also enhanced our product testing and deployment workflow."
- **Result**: The startup launched three successful dApps within six months, earning over 20,000 active users.

2. Empowering Activists in Restricted Regions

- **User**: Environmental activist in a restricted region
- **Challenge**: "Our government's internet policies made it nearly impossible to access global environmental forums and share our findings."
- **Solution**: "Mises Browser's encryption and VPN capabilities opened the door for us to connect with global networks safely."

- **Result**: The activist successfully collaborated with international organizations, leading to impactful environmental policy changes in their region.

3. An Investor's Secure Portfolio Management

- **User**: Cryptocurrency investor in Europe
- **Challenge**: "Managing multiple wallets and keeping track of my investments securely was overwhelming."
- **Solution**: "The browser's integrated wallet was a game-changer. It supported all my currencies and made transactions incredibly easy."
- **Result**: The investor increased their portfolio by 35% within a year, citing enhanced security and reduced transaction errors as key benefits.

4. A Content Creator's Productivity Boost

- **User**: YouTube creator focused on cryptocurrency education
- **Challenge**: "Ads and trackers in mainstream browsers slowed down my research process and compromised my privacy."
- **Solution**: "Switching to Mises Browser eliminated distractions and provided the privacy I needed to create quality content."
- **Result**: The creator's subscriber base grew by 50%, as viewers appreciated the depth and accuracy of their insights.

5. Educating the Next Generation of Developers

- **User**: Coding bootcamp instructor
- **Challenge**: "Introducing Web3 to students was difficult due to the lack of user-friendly tools."
- **Solution**: "Mises Browser bridged the gap, providing students with hands-on experience in interacting with dApps and blockchain networks."

- **Result**: Graduates reported higher employability in blockchain-focused roles, with many securing positions at leading tech companies.

The Future of Browsing with Mises

As we look toward the future of the internet, the role of web browsers in shaping how we interact with digital environments is becoming more critical than ever. The rise of privacy concerns, the increasing reliance on decentralized technologies, and the demand for better security in the online ecosystem are all driving the evolution of web browsers. Among the most innovative players in this space is the Mises Browser, which has positioned itself as a frontrunner in the emerging decentralized web.

The Mises Browser offers more than just privacy and security; it is a tool that embodies the future of browsing by facilitating greater control over online interactions, enabling seamless Web3 experiences, and fostering a privacy-first internet ecosystem. Here's a look at the future of browsing, powered by Mises, and how it is poised to shape the decentralized web.

Emerging Trends in Web Browsers

The world of web browsing is rapidly evolving, and several key trends are shaping the future of the online experience. Mises Browser is at the intersection of these trends, offering cutting-edge solutions to meet the demands of an increasingly decentralized and privacy-conscious internet. Some of the major trends include:

1. Decentralization and Web3 Integration

Decentralization is perhaps the most significant trend in the current web development landscape. Web3—the third iteration of the internet—is based on blockchain technology and decentralized networks that eliminate centralized control over data, applications, and services.

Unlike Web2, where data is controlled by a handful of corporate giants, Web3 offers a more open, transparent, and user-controlled internet experience.

Web browsers are evolving to support decentralized applications (dApps) and provide users with the tools they need to interact with blockchain-based networks and services. Mises Browser is at the forefront of this shift, offering seamless Web3 integration and easy access to decentralized applications.

2. Privacy-First Browsing

With data privacy becoming a top priority for internet users, privacy-first browsers are on the rise. As concerns about government surveillance, corporate data harvesting, and online tracking continue to grow, users are seeking browsers that protect their personal information. Privacy features such as encryption, anonymous browsing, and the ability to block trackers and ads are becoming essential.

Mises Browser's robust privacy tools, including its built-in VPN, ad-blocking functionality, and secure encryption, reflect this shift toward privacy-conscious browsing. As online privacy becomes more vital, Mises Browser is positioning itself as a trusted and secure option for users who value control over their data.

3. Blockchain-Powered Identity and Authentication

In the future, traditional login methods like usernames and passwords may become obsolete, replaced by blockchain-based identity systems. These systems enable users to control their digital identity securely and without relying on centralized services. The integration of decentralized identity protocols (DID) is already gaining traction in the Web3 ecosystem.

Mises Browser is poised to support this transition, offering users the ability to manage their decentralized identities directly within the browser. This will significantly reduce the risks associated with identity theft and centralized data breaches.

4. The Rise of Web3 Services

As Web3 continues to grow, an increasing number of decentralized services are emerging, spanning finance (DeFi), entertainment (NFTs), social media, and more. Traditional web browsers have limited functionality for interacting with these services, making it harder for users to engage with blockchain-powered platforms.

Mises Browser, however, is designed specifically to support Web3 services, allowing users to access dApps, NFTs, and decentralized finance platforms without friction. The integration of blockchain networks directly into the browser enhances the user experience by providing seamless interaction with the decentralized internet.

5. Artificial Intelligence and Smart Browsing

The future of browsing also lies in the incorporation of artificial intelligence (AI) to enhance browsing experiences. AI-powered browsers can personalize user experiences, streamline tasks, and automate functions, making browsing more efficient. From predictive search results to automatic privacy settings, AI will play a central role in the next generation of web browsing.

Mises Browser's forward-thinking approach includes AI-powered enhancements designed to improve browsing security, automate privacy protection, and help users navigate the decentralized web with ease.

How Mises is Shaping the Decentralized Web

Mises Browser is more than just a tool for accessing the internet; it is actively contributing to the shaping of the decentralized web. By integrating cutting-edge technologies and forward-looking features, the browser is playing a pivotal role in the evolution of Web3. Here's how Mises is helping to shape the decentralized future of the internet:

1. Facilitating Seamless Web3 Experiences

As the decentralized web continues to grow, Web3 applications will become a central part of users' daily lives. Mises Browser has been designed with Web3 integration at its core, providing users with the tools they need to engage with decentralized applications effortlessly. Whether it's interacting with decentralized finance (DeFi) platforms, using non-fungible tokens (NFTs), or exploring decentralized social networks, Mises is ensuring that users can participate in the Web3 ecosystem without barriers.

Mises is paving the way for mass adoption of decentralized applications by offering an intuitive browsing experience that connects users directly to Web3 services. With this functionality, Mises is contributing to the transition from the centralized web to a more open, user-controlled internet.

2. Protecting User Privacy in a Decentralized World

In a decentralized web, privacy becomes even more important as users take greater control over their data and digital identities. Mises Browser is built on the premise that privacy should be a fundamental right, not a luxury. Through advanced encryption, anonymous browsing modes, ad-blocking, and integrated VPN tools, Mises enables users to protect their privacy while engaging with decentralized services.

As data privacy concerns continue to mount, Mises is setting a new standard for secure and private browsing in the decentralized world. By prioritizing user privacy, Mises helps maintain the integrity of the decentralized web, ensuring that it remains a safe and trustworthy space for all users.

3. Supporting Blockchain Interoperability

A major challenge facing the decentralized web is interoperability—the ability for different blockchain networks to communicate and share data seamlessly. Mises Browser is designed to address this issue by supporting multiple blockchain networks and facilitating cross-chain communication. This enables users to interact with decentralized applications and services across different blockchains without encountering compatibility issues.

Mises Browser is enhancing the overall Web3 ecosystem by creating a more interconnected and interoperable decentralized world. As more blockchain networks emerge, Mises will continue to play a key role in ensuring that users can access and interact with a wide range of decentralized services.

4. Driving Open-Source Innovation

Mises Browser is committed to open-source development, fostering collaboration within the global developer community. By allowing developers to contribute to the project, Mises ensures that its features and capabilities evolve in line with the latest advancements in the decentralized space. This collaborative approach not only improves the browser itself but also contributes to the broader decentralized web ecosystem.

Mises Browser is driving innovation by supporting an open-source development model that encourages experimentation, collaboration, and the creation of new decentralized technologies. This will help accelerate the development of the decentralized web, making it more accessible and robust for everyone.

Glossary of Terms

1. **Ad Blocking**: The practice of preventing or blocking advertisements from appearing on websites, often to enhance user experience, improve loading times, and increase privacy.

2. **API (Application Programming Interface)**: A set of protocols and tools that allow software applications to communicate with each other. In the context of Mises Browser, APIs are used to interact with decentralized applications (dApps) and other blockchain services.

3. **Blockchain**: A decentralized, distributed ledger technology that records

transactions across multiple computers in such a way that the registered transactions cannot be altered retroactively. It is the foundational technology behind cryptocurrencies and Web3 applications.

4. **Cryptocurrency**: A digital or virtual currency that uses cryptography for security, making it difficult to counterfeit or double-spend. Popular examples include Bitcoin, Ethereum, and other altcoins.

5. **dApp (Decentralized Application)**: A type of application that runs on a decentralized network, such as a blockchain, rather than on centralized servers controlled by a single entity. dApps are often used in Web3 ecosystems for activities like finance, gaming, social media, and more.

6. **Decentralization**: The distribution of authority, control, and power away from a

central authority, typically in the context of systems like blockchain, where no single party has control over the entire network.

7. **Encryption**: The process of converting data into a code to prevent unauthorized access. Encryption is a key aspect of ensuring the privacy and security of online activities, particularly in browsers and cryptocurrency wallets.

8. **Extension**: A small software program that adds specific functionality to a web browser. Extensions can enhance user experience, add new features, and integrate additional tools such as ad blockers or password managers.

9. **Fungible Token**: A type of cryptocurrency or digital asset that is interchangeable with other tokens of the same type and value. For example, Bitcoin is fungible because each coin holds the

same value as another.

10. **dApp Store**: A platform where users can discover, download, and interact with decentralized applications. Similar to app stores for smartphones, a dApp store for a browser facilitates the distribution of Web3 applications.

11. **Hashing**: A cryptographic function that converts data into a fixed-size string of characters, which is usually a hash value. In blockchain technology, hashing ensures data integrity and security.

12. **IPFS (InterPlanetary File System)**: A peer-to-peer protocol for storing and sharing data in a distributed manner. IPFS allows for the storage of files in a decentralized way, meaning that files are not dependent on a single server or organization.

13. **Private Key**: A secret cryptographic key used in digital wallets to sign transactions and prove ownership of cryptocurrencies or digital assets. It is critical to keep a private key secure, as it grants access to the funds stored in the wallet.

14. **Public Key**: A cryptographic key that is used to receive digital assets. Unlike a private key, a public key is visible to others and does not need to be kept secret.

15. **Security Token**: A type of cryptocurrency that represents an ownership stake in a real-world asset, such as shares in a company or real estate. Security tokens are subject to regulations in many jurisdictions.

16. **Smart Contract**: A self-executing contract with the terms of the agreement directly written into code. Smart contracts run on blockchain platforms like

Ethereum and are used to automate transactions and enforce contractual terms.

17. **VPN (Virtual Private Network)**: A service that encrypts internet traffic and hides a user's IP address to improve online privacy and security. VPNs are often used to access restricted content or to browse the web anonymously.

18. **Web3**: The third iteration of the internet, which focuses on decentralization, blockchain technology, and user control over data. Web3 enables applications and services to run on decentralized networks, offering more privacy, transparency, and user empowerment compared to Web2.

19. **WebSocket**: A communication protocol that allows for full-duplex communication channels over a single TCP connection. WebSockets are used in

real-time applications, such as those
involving cryptocurrency transactions and
dApps.

20.   **Wallet Address**: A unique identifier
associated with a user's digital wallet,
allowing them to send and receive
cryptocurrencies. A wallet address is
typically represented as a string of
alphanumeric characters.

21.   **White Paper**: A detailed report or
guide that presents the objectives,
technologies, use cases, and
implementation plans of a project. White
papers are common in blockchain and
cryptocurrency projects, as they outline
the vision and goals of a new technology
or platform.

22.   **Tokenomics**: The economic model
behind a cryptocurrency or token,
including its supply, distribution, and
incentive structure. Tokenomics is an

important consideration for users when evaluating the potential success and value of a cryptocurrency project.

23.   **Blockchain Fork**: A split in the blockchain protocol, which can result in two separate versions of the blockchain. Forks can occur for a variety of reasons, such as disagreements among developers or the need to implement new features.

24.   **NFT (Non-Fungible Token)**: A unique digital asset that represents ownership or proof of authenticity of a specific item or piece of content, such as artwork, music, or virtual goods. NFTs are often bought, sold, and traded on blockchain networks.

25.   **Node**: A participant in a decentralized network, typically a computer that helps validate and propagate transactions within a blockchain. Nodes are crucial to the functioning of blockchain and Web3

ecosystems.

26.   **PoW (Proof of Work)**: A consensus mechanism used by certain blockchain networks (like Bitcoin) to validate transactions and secure the network. PoW requires participants (miners) to solve complex cryptographic puzzles to add new blocks to the blockchain.

27.   **PoS (Proof of Stake)**: An alternative consensus mechanism to Proof of Work, where validators (stakers) are selected to create new blocks based on the amount of cryptocurrency they hold and are willing to "stake" as collateral.

28.   **Decentralized Identity (DID)**: A new model for managing digital identities, where individuals can own and control their own identities without relying on a central authority. DID systems use blockchain or distributed ledger technology to store and verify identity

information.

29. **Transaction Fee**: A small fee paid to the network (miners or validators) to process and confirm a transaction. Transaction fees are often associated with blockchain-based activities such as cryptocurrency transfers or smart contract executions.

30. **Cold Storage**: A method of storing cryptocurrencies offline to protect them from hacks or unauthorized access. Cold storage is typically used for long-term storage and involves hardware wallets or paper wallets.

31. **Hot Wallet**: A digital wallet connected to the internet, which allows for quick access and transaction capabilities. Hot wallets are more convenient but are also more vulnerable to hacks compared to cold storage solutions.

32. **Token Swap**: The process of exchanging one type of cryptocurrency or token for another, typically done through decentralized exchanges or directly within Web3 applications.

33. **Gas Fees**: The transaction fees required to perform actions on a blockchain, particularly on the Ethereum network. Gas fees are paid to miners or validators to incentivize them to process and validate transactions.

34. **MetaMask**: A popular cryptocurrency wallet and browser extension that enables users to interact with decentralized applications (dApps) and manage their digital assets on the Ethereum blockchain.

35. **IPV6**: The most recent version of the Internet Protocol (IP) that provides a larger address space and improved security features compared to the older IPv4. It is designed to accommodate the

growing number of devices connected to the internet.

36.   **Peer-to-Peer (P2P)**: A type of network where users interact directly with one another, sharing resources and data without relying on a central server. Many Web3 applications use P2P technology for decentralized file storage and communication.

37.   **Sharding**: A method used to scale blockchains by dividing the network into smaller pieces, or "shards," which can process transactions in parallel. Sharding helps improve the speed and efficiency of blockchain networks.

38.   **DAO (Decentralized Autonomous Organization)**: An organization that operates based on smart contracts and decentralized governance, where decisions are made by token holders rather than centralized leadership. DAOs are

commonly used in Web3 ecosystems to govern projects and communities.

39.   **Immutable**: Refers to data or content that cannot be changed, altered, or deleted once it has been recorded. In blockchain technology, transactions and records are immutable, ensuring their integrity and security.

40.   **Layer 2 Solutions**: Protocols built on top of a blockchain to improve scalability and reduce transaction costs. Layer 2 solutions are designed to process transactions off-chain while still ensuring the security of the underlying blockchain.

Ultimate Mises Browser Bible

Ultimate Mises Browser Bible

www.ingramcontent.com/pod-product-compliance
Lightning Source LLC
Chambersburg PA
CBHW071208050326
40689CB00011B/2279